THAT WE HAVE LIVED AT ALL

That We Have Lived At All

poems of love, witness & gratitude

Marilyn Lerch

Chapel Street Editions

Copyright © 2018 by Marilyn Lerch
All rights reserved

Published by
Chapel Street Editions
150 Chapel St.
Woodstock, New Brunswick E7M 1H4
www.chapelstreeteditions.com

ISBN 978-1-988299-19-8

Library and Archives Canada Cataloguing in Publication

Title: That we have lived at all : poems of love, witness & gratitude / Marilyn Lerch.
Other titles: Poems of love, witness & gratitude
Names: Lerch, Marilyn, author.
Identifiers: Canadiana 2018906823X | ISBN 9781988299198 (softcover)
Classification: LCC PS8573.E657 T53 2018 | DDC C811/.54—dc23

Book design by Brendan Helmuth

Photo of the author by Janet Hammock

Dedication

For Janet

&

for you who rise each morning to grieve and resist the continuing desecration of Earth and its myriad and wondrous life forms by human institutions mired in greed, domination and indifference.

Contents

Foreword i

Part I: Close To Home
   When I Knew I Would Stay 3
   Your Hoisted Heart Flies Wild Tonight 5
   Fire and Ice 7
   Threnody at White Point, Cape Breton, Late September 2001 9
   Thaw on High Marsh Road 11
   Choose One Tree and Love It 12
   Trans 13
   Poet's Retreat on Panmure Island 14
   Out Rockport Way 18
   For the Sheer Joy I 24

Part II: I Want You To Know About This
   I Want You to Know About This 27
   Dissolution, Anyone? 29
   Family Romance 30
   Waiting 31
   Tantramar 32
   Tantramar Towers, Radio Canada International 33
   Ode to a Plain Saucer 34
   Not Quite Right 36
   Perspectivo 37
   Rethinking Cremation 38
   Letter Found in a Bottle: Is it Yours? 39
   For the Sheer Joy II 41

Part III: Recycling Samuel Beckett
    Recycling Samuel Beckett 45

Part IV: In These Anthropocene Times
    What Do You Have to Say for Yourself, Poet? 55
    Time Shaving 58
    With the Famous Five on Parliament Hill: Post Iraq Shock
        and Awe, 2004 59
    Rights of the Person Corporate 61
    If We're So Smart 62
    Murder on the Internet 64
    Election(s) November 2016 65
    In These Times 66
    The Last Luddite Addresses the Lonely Vapourized Crowd 68
    For the Sheer Joy III 72

Part V: Lines For Lines: Five Poems & Eight Gestations
    Prologue 75
    Wo(man) Standing Serene 77
    Man and Woman on a Bed 78
    Drawn to Tenderness 79
    Standing Man Leaning Forward, Arms Outstretched, Head Hung 80
    Man and Woman with Wings 81
    Eight Gestations 82
    For the Sheer Joy IV 84

Part VI: Foremothers
    Foremothers 86
    For the Sheer Joy V 98

Note 99
Acknowledgements 99
About the Author 101

Foreword

"There is a line among the fragments of the Greek poet Archilochus which says, 'The fox knows many things, but the hedgehog knows one big thing.'"

This is the opening sentence of Isaiah Berlin's essay on Tolstoy, *The Hedgehog and the Fox*, in which he discusses two contrasting approaches taken by philosophers and poets for understanding life and history. The richness of literature derives from the fact that some writers bend one way and some the other in their efforts to express the way things are for them in the world.

Some writers have a talent for bending both ways. This fertile mix of attention to detail and the gift of holistic vision goes a long way to explain the beauty and power of Marilyn Lerch's new book of poetry.

There is a core vision here that informs the life and work of this poet. It repeatedly bursts forth with incisive images of the human world she cares about so deeply and with which she has a long history of passionate engagement. These images characterize both the insufferable folly that now threatens the commonwealth of life, and her unwavering commitment to a shared vision of how to make a better world for all.

But, at the same time, there are poems in this book that tread so delicately, and with such precise interest in the details of things and the nuances of relationships, that only the nose of a "fox" could have picked them up for savouring and recording. It's hard to say which orientation lies at the poetic heart of this book, but taken together they weave a rich fabric of celebration for the fact "that we have lived at all."

Through it all she retains a vital connection with the beauty of the Earth and a compassionate hold on the reality of both personal and community relationships. We are fortunate indeed to have this testament of "love, witness, and gratitude" from a writer who is not shy of wading into the dark complexity of the world, and, at the same time, is willing to hold up the illumination of her poetic practice as a gift to her readers.

Keith Helmuth
Chapel Street Editions
Woodstock, New Brunswick
November 2018

Part I
Close To Home

When I Knew I Would Stay

When I knew I would stay
and someone wanted me to stay,
when I was given hangers and space,
and had alphabetized my books,
when like a strong articulated wing
I was at last connected and free, then
could I venture forth,
walk the land where everything was new:
> the nameless varieties of grasses on the marsh,
> spring manure heavy in the air,
> autumn blueberry fields turning impossibly red,
> tamaracks a golden procession into winter,
> tidal creeks, lake, bay and ocean close,
> and snow, snow, snow.

So much to explore:
> British Settlement Road to its dead end,
> the trail beyond Slack's Cove,
> the long hill into Memramcook Valley,
> bike path out to Midgic,
> the quiet at St. Anne's church.

Learning to pronounce Shimogue, Miramichi,
that boats from Bermuda had docked at Sackville,
singing new melodies to old carols and hymns,
meeting six people I know on the way to the post office,
having Acadian and MicMaq friends,
watching the children of friends grow up.
It was childhood revisited in delight and abandon
and I wanted to say everything.
No wonder a piece of driftwood became

"a god supine serene
on iron juts of rock,
the wind and tide
whorling and writing you,
silver illumined script,
how one wing fully spread
anchors you in red mud."
No wonder
that the shaping forces of childhood,
ambivalent mother and a father lost to himself,
the desperate need and fear of family
became clarified in this salt sea air.
I finally wore through a pair of shoes
I'd walked in forever
and feet touched ground.
The beauty of two
could flower into one…
one full moon shared at Beausejour and Mikanos,
one confluence, only the flow and
coming to serenity in the flow.

Your Hoisted Heart Flies Wild Tonight

For Linda Dornan

Your hoisted heart flies wild tonight
Wind-whipped above the gallery,
red dementia against the storm-purple sky,
a nylon hyperbole of valves and ventricles
that turns snow to blood,
an open-ended heart so as not to break.
Inside, the (in)tangible evidence
 subverts the familiar, dislocates language
to the thinking body:
    a porcelain heart flute,
     two interlocking pelvic bones
      that share a mouth,
    a chocolate tongue,
    a glass harp holding silence.
No wonder then that your beloved
seizes the moment and shaping love
 to what his brain allows
in full-voiced splendour
la la la's his heart out.
Did you know all along that your art
was preparing you for life,
ephemeral, decontextualized, a perpetual letting go?
How wonderful.
Not easy, though,
all those years of care giving,
waking each morning
to a shifting actor on a shifting stage.
In a sudden hiatus of wind,

the heart sags against the pole.
You know more than most
what it means to be empty,
what it means to be joyful.
        By the sea somewhere at dusk,
        you walked into the surf,
        your ankle looped by a rope staked in sand,
        and dragged baggage onshore, keening,
        telling stories
                of Irish arrivals.
You've always shown
how much freedom
a tethered heart can have,
and oh,
with such poignancy
how he(art) is made.

Fire and Ice

        In Memory of Jamie Gripton

He pursued the puck
as if God were in it,
made to be whacked home,
Score!

The Rev was
all glory and affirmation,
ordained in comradery,
fearless competitor and playful,
his loves ferocious, Cohen
and Dylan and justice;
one speed, all out,
whether wielding the hockey stick or
a machete.
Yes, he did that once
in Tim Hortons
while reading a Jamaican poem,
just one of the Rovers;
happened a plainclothes cop,
sipping a double double,
suggested, "That's a lethal weapon, guy,"
and Jamie sheathed his zeal,
only time.

God in his grip or gripped by God,
same thing,
kneeling in prayer—
"Jesus, can't we move things along faster,"

or on his knees reciting a love poem
to an elderly Drew resident,
same thing;
a hipster minister,
down to earth and far out.

Once on Christmas Eve,
we stopped by the Upper Sackville church,
wood stove ablaze,
and Jamie in white robe and rainbow doublet
welcomed us,
his eyes joy-brimming
as if angels had descended,
that's how he made you feel,
good and worthy.

Cancer whacked him
and he lay for months in bed,
not forsaken but
speaking of Suzanne at the river
and matters philosophic with an old friend.
Then,
he moved out,
left Christine and the girls,
moved into
a seriously whimsical eternity
where our minds end
and Jamie's God
begins.

Threnody at White Point, Cape Breton, Late September 2001

The wooing wind and sea on the way to the point
like a strummed fundamental deep in the chest,
throat's grief, its fifth above.

What do we know of invisible shoals,
      of ugly juts of rocks beneath the waves,
as innocent of what lies ahead
      as these dozen sailors buried here
who hailed land's sight
      and perished soon thereafter.
          But   look   how those green buoys   lilt
             and bob   tilt tip to lip   of swell
                wave-swamped   pressed low to horizontal
          how they up-spring   wagging fingers at fate

A cove, sea-carved from rock,
sea-motion smoothing erratics elliptic,
dense poundage layered on the slanting beach,
the surge, narrowing between portals,
gathers strength, drags leaden eggs
rumbling over themselves,
the powerful counter pull in its foamy residue
rattles and clatters, stone against stone.

          The rocky projection
          ends abruptly,
          vertical to the churning sea;
          behind on a hill a stranger looms,
          crowding my thoughts to the edge.

Here, among the natural headstones of the sailors' cemetery,
one roughly shaped,
perhaps by an old mariner, safe from the sea's reach
who witnessed a broken, unclaimed body lowered in the ground
and moved by kindred feel for heaving decks and groaning wood,
lifted and placed this heavy stone.

                See   how that niched light
        takes   the brunt of   hammer wind
                    cascading sheets
            rebounding ever upright
                green saint in her   outermost station
          anchored deep   and holding

An unknown sailor beneath the stones,
one lone cormorant on the darkening sea,
one swan far behind the flock;
        go brothers, seek and find the others,
        seek and find the others.

Thaw on High Marsh Road

Fog muffles the dawn,
so dense it smudges a cow's low moan,
dulls distant hammer blows,
here and there a barn
levitates in grayness.
December's many snowfalls,
fluffy enough to shovel with one hand,
become this morning's stand-still flood,
fields of fenced-in water,
ditches full,
the air breathing,
Tantramar afloat.

Choose One Tree and Love It

There's an oak tree on Charles Street
whose branches stretch in all directions,
intent on taking space into itself.
At Bridge and Brooks
a maple is the first to catch fire,
autumnal flame in every leaf.
Choose one tree and love it.
Mine, the copper beech
on the grounds of the Civic Centre,
fagus syulvatica purpurea,
planted in the 1930's
where the Dominion Seed Company used to be.
I approach as I would a sacred place,
circumambulate in twenty-four small steps,
its massive trunk
wrinkled like elephant hide and pocked
with sunburst fungi and black moss.
For ninety years this stone hard tree
has been ringing outward,
thrusting upward,
its roots spreading, going deep
to stabilize the enormous weight.
Nine muscular primary branches
create its dark green, near perfect canopy
and its growing is not done,
not yet begun
that descent through generations of us
into pungent rot.
There's still time
to choose one tree and love it.

Trans

The baker doesn't have her story
but knows what he sees
"Thank you, m'am."
That's all she needs,
appearances are everything.
I am woman. Enough.

Through half a life-time,
marriage, family, profession,
staked to an old family name,
she'd been kept out of sight.
No way to come to term
without coming to terms,
without turning inside out,
doing away with appearances.

She walks down the street,
a little hitch in her stride.
People pass and nod or stop to talk,
share photos of grandchildren.

I am woman,
that's my story,
can't get enough of being seen.

Poet's Retreat on Panmure Island

I
Thunder rumbles here,
a gentle rolling preamble,
faint tremors of lightning
shimmering
behind night clouds.
I send the first cooling drops,
ask you to fall with
one—
from such a height!—
imagine its integrity
released
momentarily
from the all-
consuming abstraction,
and then we may begin
the "far more difficult business"
said Virginia Woolf
"of intimacy."

II
On the first day the ocean was roused and furious,
waves rushing in on themselves
gathering   breaking hard
every four seconds   I counted   around my legs.
A few steps more and my whole self
would feel the force,
but I had promised the one
who knows how the sea draws me,

so for love's sake
I crossed the causeway,
and stepped into the placid sandy-bottomed bay,
imagining the last second dive,
the power sliding
harmlessly over my back.

III
It's quiet and cold in the cabin this morning,
a miniature high rise heater slowly oscillates the only warmth,
and during each swivel
of its glassed in, reflecting, red hot vertical core,
one becomes many becomes one becomes
mesmerizing;
one bright ribbon a curtain of ribbons,
one electric red fish a squiggling swarm
as heat leaves my knees,
returns and leaves,
returns…

IV
Panmure Island belongs
to itself again,
even the ocean lays down.
The trickle of tourists across the causeway
ceased on Labour Day
so it's just
Atticus Finch, Ellie, Sharon Lucy, Michael, Nudge and Tony
two dogs, two people, two cats
alone or easily mingling,
with that scribbler down the lane.

V
coyotes pierce the night sky
yelping at Ursa Major
as close to a bear as they'll get
or a deer   or a moose
on all of PEI

VI
The wind a bit of a moan today
between the ocean and the bay,
I coast, foot off pedal,
from the paved road—
keep going, keep going—
to end of Blueberry Lane,
ever the child.
The sun comes out,
Atticus Finch comes in
wagging a few images,
pretty much what happens
at Artist's Way.

VII
Tony was born
with three legs,
his gait unmistakable,
natural and sufficient;
so different if you come
whole into the world
expecting to remain so,
and suddenly you are
just a phantom arm
reaching for the jam.

VIII
North wind riffles the bay
sending riplets aslant toward shore
first touch,
an acute angle
then lacy lines
closing down to zero
touching
rippling
closing
soft eye gazing
mesmerized.

IX
The wind is up,
sun on water.
I know you are the sun
and I the water,
what, my darling, shall we call
the wind
that creates our glittering dance?

Out Rockport Way

I
Rockport is not
    a port
    not a town or even a village.
It has no sidewalks,
no store windows or municipal laws to break,
lots of rocks though.
Rockport is
    a rattling bridge over a tidal creek,
    some abandoned shacks off in the woods,
    a few families, a few loners,
    moose and wind, bear and wind, deer and wind.

II
Down the steep hill to Slack's Cove,
I see a truck mired in mud, a man
waving me back,
so I visit the cemetery instead.
A grinding stone stands heavily at the entrance
where rest the Kings and Towers,
and a few lyrical Delesderniers.
One rough, chalky white headstone
makes me wonder
who was left to chisel the names:
    Mary Jane,
    Daughter of Milledge and Dorothy Tower,
    Died November 27, 1859 at…
    letters worn to blank indentations;
    Luliah Deliah,

December 3, 1859, at four years of life;
Henrietta,
her name half sunk in the ground,
all those years of unlived life bearing down.

III
Beyond Slack's Cove,
the gravel road enters the woods
and narrows to rutted, grass-trampled tracks.
Tree roots, raised like old veins,
bear the weight of boots and heavy tires
belonging to those
who have some business here.
New bricks strewn and old bricks
sunk subliminal
hold the semblance of a trail
that others also travel on.
Always a sighing
of wind and water,
becoming one.
Trees shoulder close on both sides,
rags of bearded moss drift like gray haze,
green moss thickens everywhere,
a rise in the path closes what's beyond,
more eyes watching than can be known.

IV
Along the road from Sackville out Rockport way,
there used to be hand-made signs tacked to fence posts:
Ancient Grave Site, Wilbur's Tea Room, Stone Chimney Lookout.
And though the grave was unmarked,

the tea room closed, the chimney hard to find,
no matter;
just the comfort of land known,
every contour and cove once walked.

V
Once I set myself the task of going out often
to where the rattling bridge crosses the creek
and a beach sprawls under cliffs,
there to mark the changes through seasons.
Death interrupted but that is another story.

September
> A breeze riffles expectations and moths,
> fragile on the warm air.
> Tucked and motionless gulls float
> on the outward moving tidal sheen.
> Apples strew the beach far
> > from their falling place.
> Rooted on the cliff tops,
> mountain ash, apple and birch
> bend to the curve of erosion,
> pebbles clatter down randomly

> > October
> > > Yellowish-brown waves curl and slap-whoosh the shore,
> > > almost touching my shadow, sun deep in my back.
> > > Nearby, a sandpiper cozies down in a bowl of fine shale.
> > > The moon setting somewhere draws out the slap-whoosh
> > > > to just a whisper.

        Smoked white sky,
        light rain, warm and
        no horizons,
        turning desire in
        on itself.
        Apples soften around their core
        Shallow waves splash, retreat
        and meet another,
            nudging
        reeds to sway on themselves.

November
    The body of water has disappeared,
    pulled by moon and tide
    through winding slick red mud canyons.

        Under foot,
        miniature landscapes of gray spongy clay
        hold trembling pools,
        the least drop shimmering.

            Sunset smudged,
            enough light to dye the beach
            deep rose going
            mahogany on the way back,
            crunch of shale,
            whisperbrush of down jacket.

Late November
        The tide's slow insinuation under the bridge,
        Heavy between mud banks,
        a muscled musing into the woods,

                silty ochre and iron-tinted designs
                move on its moving,
                mandalas, languid dragons,
                coastlines being undone.

        Apples strewn since September along the high tide line,
        wrinkled skins curled in straw and seaweed.

December
Noon of Winter Solstice,
day and seasons divide,
the prune-purple beach partitions
pale yellow sea grass from a fresh line of snow.
        And here,
        water gushes over a cliff,
        a manic slippage down
        behind a transparent staircase of ice,
        spurt-gurgles through holes
        in the shiny red shale.

                A frozen landscape
                except for the narrow stream winding
                out, out
                into mother body
                and my tromping on the hard mud floor
                out, out
                to the end of the sky.

January
        Two weeks of freeze and the waves
        have been startled, stymied mid-gesture
        in motionless heaps and jumble.

February
> Three layers of frosted snow, a geological cross-section runs through
> the thick ice shelf, fissured and broken along the shore,
> evidence of one Alberta clipper and two blizzards in seven days.

And then, on February 28, 2005, Gwen died;
my next-to-last farewell, a bow from the door,
and she bowing back.
"Love you," I said, everyone did.
Too soon, only ninety-three,
Life of the party, most gracious and lovely,
Bowing out of this world.

> In the dead of night on a bus leaving Holguin.
> A black pig trots out of a ditch into the headlights
> and back again.
> Those who knew Gwen well will understand
> why we call this her second farewell.

And for a while, I had no heart for Rockport.

For the Sheer Joy I

late October, low three o'clock sun deepens the sunglass colours of the
back yard garden—green gone coppery, russet, smoky topaz – where
faint mint and lavender linger and something pungently tropical
torpors the air, where a desultory sag and droop prevails, ragged
head-heavy sunflowers depleted of seeds bend from the waist, hostas
collapse into plush golden skirts, while only the most fragile cosmos
still surge to bloom on those thin, resilient, outward bound stems,
and a few coneflowers glow cinnamon before succumbing to big-eyed
ebony spiders; insects enter a sun zone fluttering shadows on the
house siding, and most delighting: on the inside of transparent reddish
Rhododendron leaves, shadows hang, reflective of other leaves and in a
corner ghost-writing itself, a whitish gray lacy astilbe.

Part II
I Want You To Know About This

I Want You to Know About This

I want you to know about this,
how, whenever I close my eyes,
it's not to darkness
but to images rising
resolving, dissolving,
one into another,
unbidden, unwilled.

How faces—
most often strangers–
swim into my rapt gaze
looking beyond me
in detail so finely drawn
the seeing is touching,
or locking eyes in
sudden intimacy.

How this supple spaciousness
behind, before my eyes
shiftshapes
smiles into grief,
anguish into joy.

How sometimes I move bodiless
down damp stone stairs,
through winding passageways,
swirl down whirlpools,
fly low over landscapes, eagle-eyed,
out to horizons.

I care not how they come to be,
let science plot my brain;
just know
this ephemeral gallery,
these processionals
without plot or theme,
rhyme or reason,
exist.
Whenever
I close my eyes
it's never to darkness.

Dissolution, Anyone?

I've always loved that slow modulation into sleep,
the falling
from one world into another.

On a front porch in Vancouver,
two quick drags
on some powerful dope
and words come cottony
from great distances,
my hungry brain begins fending
for itself,
and I retire inside the spectacle
unfolding for hours;
waves towering, breaking
deliciously
over my skull,
colours and shapes in slow motion
convolutions
"Are you OK?" the friendly inquiry.
Languidly,
"I could live like this."

And then those few
pre-colonoscopy moments
in a cold room
when the fluid enters
and I watch myself fade out,
returning as a dreamy pond floater
intoning, "Dr. Shakarinia is so wonderful."
Leaving the world
is not such a bad thing
as long as I ....

Family Romance

My father used to say
about anything requiring effort,
"Why bother?" or "To hell with it,"
revealing a profound lethargy
or a latent Zen tendency
which, taken together,
pretty well described
how he loved me.
I'd show mine
by standing on the mound
in the dining room,
winding up, casting a wary eye to first,
and burning a fastball through the
sunroom window.

Waiting

I'm waiting
in the arrival area.
Arrivals happen here.
Having turned 80,
I should have by now,
not as in "she's finally made it",
but a rocking chair equanimity.

I'm waiting
in the arrival area;
haven't I always been?
Those old shadow fears
of being left
stymie my leaving or
send me chasing time;
either way, I remain in place.
Now you understand.
Flip the coin,
it never falls.

You have to leave to arrive,
have to wait to arrive.
I manage both at once;
where that leaves me is
up in the air
under the schedule board
flashing
en retarde.

Tantramar

This is the land I'll die in,
love-rooted for the last time,
where rivers end as narrow seepages into the ground,
last landscape to know
like the tributaries of my hand,
seeing it anew until I'm
residual of dust at Four Corners.

Not unwelcome, these thoughts slip in
a mild December day, ice tentative
in tractor ruts, snow
yet to fall on blueberry rust,
last roads I'll walk all seasons through,
offering poems of hay and marsh, wind and tide
to make myself familiar,
though always from away.
Tantramar,
place most loved,
last home of my coming to terms,
in-gathering love, holding dear
and lightly the final ebbing away.

Tantramar Towers, Radio Canada International

Remember those nights
when snow swirled 'round the car
and cresting Beech Hill you saw
those red lights flashing "not far, not far."

Remember those bus rides home
after losing a tough road game
and someone yelled, "There they are!"
and all was possible again;
or stepping from the train
so long, so long away,
to see those towers standing
natural as the marsh or bay.

Remember the many ways
we were welcomed home
all seasons, all day, all night.

All gone.

Ode to a Plain Saucer

Amiga,
you suffer
like anything made incomplete,
an oarlock without oar.
All need and separation,
your grooves circle an emptiness,
your destiny in other hands.
But listen, we're something like you,
longing for fulfillment and
love, of course.
Once you heard of an object
with your name
that travels light years
toward desire and
sometimes you fling yourself
into that night void,
anything better than
this static, stacked condition.
Then comes the rattle, the bustle
and you are in the sun
with the one and only,
the perfect fit,
and it is filled
and you are filled,
stirred and stirred
until
your cup runneth over,
and then you are rinsed clean
and empty again.

But Amiga,
how fortunate to know
what you are beholden to,
whereas our tragedy
is emerging from and returning to
that cold night void.

Not Quite Right

The woman was
not quite right,
how we say of
anything off kilter,
slightly awkward,
like the small bird this winter
who appeared under the feeder
hopping, pecking black seeds,
stopping now and then
to flutter one wing.
The woman
would begin a story,
trail off
into a hurt, small smile.
I watched the bird all afternoon
going through the motions;
with coming dark
it sheltered under the spruce hedge
to wait,
shorn
like the woman
of all that made sense.

Perspectivo

Mr. Brush, yes, our sixth grade art teacher, tall, bald, distantly pleasant, tried to teach us perspective without mention of Brunelleschi, which might have helped, or how creating depth in two-dimensions was revolutionary, or how once something catches on no one can escape it, like families, when a new girl entered the class, Phyllis, her name, early maturing, large-boned, shy, who soon thereafter let go a fart, allowing us a false perspective, a brief release from walking the plank to Mr. Brush's desk exhibiting our un-mastery until with a check mark we could leave the vanishing point behind forever, but poor Phyllis went and went, her virgin sheet becoming murkier and murkier, until cheek and fingers smudged, working her way toward the horizon in darkness, those attempts at foreshortening disappeared under a blackened storm cloud.

Half a century later, remembering that image, I threw myself on the bed laughing and couldn't stop, the other image there, but overshadowed, of the entire class standing, two or three on each step of an indoor wooden creaking stairway leading we hoped to Phyllis' birthday party which certainly would have absolved her of setting off a fart, and we waited and waited, she appearing at the top of the stairs every so often, that shy smile becoming darker and darker with shame, an angry male voice behind her, until finally in tears she told us to go away, and no, I don't remember what became of her or even the next day in school, but how I laughed helplessly at that black-clouded sheet of paper walking by my desk.

Rethinking Cremation

Heat has never bothered me much
but lately I've begun to rethink cremation;
a rough pine box is more appealing
or one shaped like a canoe—
another codicil.
Then, there's the green peace option,
rotting in a gunny sack around the roots of a tree;
a lot more activity,
more company composing on my decomposing,
which is not all declension,
there's some extension,
nails and hair.
Oh, what the hell,
forget enclosures of any kind—
another codicil–
just leave my eyes open to the stars,
and I
will take care of the rest.

Letter Found in a Bottle: Is it Yours?

He retired last year and I'm the only one
to hear, hear, hear him.
He would not, would not ever move
when I asked him to for the children's sake.
His home, his yard, his, his, his
and mine when I couldn't move him for thirty years.

Evergreens I planted grew,
five children grew,
grown, all gone, but one challenged son,
even this he blames me for.
And then, and then,
he sold our home, made me sign,
some folks from the projects, he thought,
moving in next door
and a barking dog left by a dead neighbour.
I called the children together
to make him see, and
damn devil magician,
he went to emergency
with kidney pains.

Made me leave,
leave the framework of my life,
my trees, their peace
and move a mile away.
The car heads home,
I use the old address.
He's really messed me up.
"Divorce him," my mother says.
But he'd follow with demands.

I have no money, no training.
Not my home,
no place for my stuff.
I never get to read a sentence
without his interrupting,
never get to hear my music,
sew in peace.

I understand how women go crazy.
Early sixties and I knew of no help.
My mother had just "found herself"
and had no time for me.
So I nursed the children and evergreens,
spent twenty years in therapy,
a loveless marriage.
What's it all about? My house taken
by force, by lies, by his fears, for his sake.
That a husband can do do do this to his wife…
Death's been a welcome shadow for a long time.
I did not need to be this old to learn
that I can never, never go home.

For the Sheer Joy II

the north wind lags, then accelerates suddenly like shots of
adrenalin, gusts exploding, driving snow horizontally, a pulse
rhythmic as the ninth wave, creating a sculpture in motion on
the driveway, empty spaces and curvatures of accumulating
snow shape the elongated, dangling body of a seahorse, its
belly mounded enough to catch each wind burst sending
strands like smoke, like ghosts, scurrying, swirling clockwise
in perfect circles, perfect ellipses, back to the belly, white
traces of geometries momentarily left in black space, all day
until the seahorse sinks beneath its sea snow home.

Part III
Recycling Samuel Beckett

Recycling Samuel Beckett

Beckett saw it coming
left us
waiting
between acts
of greater or lesser catastrophe
no apocalypse
no apotheosis
die is cast
earth turns red with blood and heat
don't kid ourselves
that's what we do
waiting@go.com

Beckett had womb memories
    born expelled
        loved his mamma so
            confining confounding
                tried to escape with his life
                      impossible
                                in
                                deed
                          lived through
                      Easter uprising
                London depression
            Wars
              the one to end all
            resisted the second
        once when a knife wound
    just missed his heart
chaos found home

everything in pieces flux and flotsam shufflers shuffling millions east millions west enemies comrades passing unknown same stink same shuffle same sacks dragged heading homeless

enlightenment's noble sentiments sewer sediments running sores of Europe old body of assumptions broken on Auschwitz old domes of belief head lamps purging darkness shattered at Hiroshima poles of old world subject object unfixed skull stares world stares stare agape seeing eye to eye impossible and nothing taken for granted any order finality arbitrary cowardly human veneer

History no matter of fact rational flow of cause and effect
though death was rationalized producing unuse value
perpetrator reborn in victim turntable turns tables
something elemental at work
machine in the ghost
write the mess

Beckett didn't go absurd or existential
    both assumed a subject
never entertained nihilism
    for nothing ends
despair too self-ish
didn't go mad
or end it all
what then?
write the mess

Joyce said
    I can do anything I want
    with language
    and Beckett said

       I can do
       nothing
       with language
       and
       did nothing
       new

In the face of horrors
expansiveness obscene
he went lean, contractive
strip-searched language
pared, gnawed away
to barely barest
a and b say this
b and c the opposite
in M. A. D.
whole works do that
undoing the doing
doing the undoing

On cusp of total deconstruction
       fiction suspect comfort food force fed certainty
           underwriting Beckett
                left omnipotent author fruitless
                language
                losing itself
                in mostly silence
plot thinned to rote gestures sans consequence sans context
bodies in slow decrepitude ever moving nowhere
            didn't fall for
            take the fall for
            images

Murmuring the tedium in medium of unknowing narrator
sloughs itself almost fizzling out
narrates need to not have need to narrate
 can't go on will go on saying just enough
to leave a stain upon the silence
poignancy beyond tears   but
                in imagination found a temporary stay against chaos

dimming down down
dimmer
how dimmest dim be
and still be clear
enough to snuff
that fatuous little light on
all will be known
one day

surfaces
lives lived
bored
Sam
deeper
to almost
the irreducible
mud
realm of non-particulate
and voice
in solitary
with everyone
toe to head
over
vast tracts

dragging the old sacks
us the hell

Beckett got over God but not the absence, Bible and Dante in hip pocket
wrote
"Agape in unseen face.
That the flaw?"
Made love feast
anyhow
in the garden
couldn't help himself
did
for hobos, clowns
common plodders
us

failure
a success
making sense
bad faith
how it is
take it
and live it
by continual invention/rejection of self-invented world
otherunwise wild despair and numbing illusion
longed for grace to breathe that void know happiness
impossible in deed
Don't kid ourselves that's what we do

All critical lances draw Beckett's blood and no consensus
                                              laughter from the wings

When reader becomes the voice
and theatre goer utters the scream
when each identifies with
all
in same boat
then Sam
did write
nothing
new

Before long
and short of it
for the foreseeable
waiting mode
will give way
to people shuffling
to higher ground
away from the sea which follows
ours
a world
where not all the dead
will be buried
not all languages
and song birds
heard again
not all tribes
and thick-furred mammals
returning
not all the Earth
unearthed
but
before long

and short of it
people will stop passing
like the old buffalo herds and flights of carrier pigeons for days across
the landscape
and
settle again
no choice in the matter
for better or worse
                                  murmurs from off stage

let's leave him there
his day is done undone
ours closing faster
to an almost utmost
nigh gnaw nohow
can't go on
somehow
will go on
don't kid ourselves
that's what we do

Part IV
In These Anthropocene Times

What Do You Have to Say for Yourself, Poet?

In these times
when so much is ending,
when what is lost
will not return,
Poet,
what do you have to say for yourself?

I say
the turning point is past,
the worst is yet to come.
Having clawed to the pinnacle
we see
the ruins strewn below,
what made them
powers
the rapid descent,
so find a clear running brook
and say your goodbyes.

I say
we know we cannot go on like this
and we know it will go on like this.
We know what must be done
and we know it will not be done,
not in time, not in time,
so listen to a songbird and weep.
Weather watches
change to warnings everywhere.
Poets change warnings
into prophecies
revealing a time when

all predictions,
all fictions,
all disharmonies,
all lies,
are possible;
so fall on your knees
before the last elephant.

When science devises
a computer chip-sized space craft
attached by a laser beam
to a thin sail-like membrane
accelerated to twenty percent
the speed of light,
while babies bloat and die,
and the obscenely rich
have themselves frozen
to sit out a rough patch,
I say
climb a tree
and watch the wild go.
The 21st century is already a museum
of the too many
living useless, living dispossessed
on short fuses of rage and suffering
the common denominator,
a pitiless system.
Technique
is its own context,
eats its own tail,
squeezing culture
to a pulp.

I say
Earth has become a tightly wound
hyper-dense nervous system
of trillions of connections
whose malfunctioning
can trip-start chaos anywhere.
This is our story
whose claims will continue
many generations down.

And yet,
and yet I say
because the collapse is upon us,
because accepting the unacceptable is no longer
an option for our species,
we are called to heroic acts,
to live within
the great acceleration of fire and advancing waters,
the desperate eyes of animals and children,
with some grace and
always resistance;
to suffer, fall, fail, keep on,
sing   play   paint
write
dream
our truths.

I say
how much, what, who ends,
yet to be known.
Seeds of goodness,
seeds of courage
still being sown.

Time Shaving

So far,
we've managed
to pare time
down to
septo, femto, atto, and
yoctoseconds
One trillionth of a trillionth of a second,
one quadrillionth of a second,
whatever.
What on earth experiences anything in
00.00.00.00.00.00.00.00.00.00.00.00.00.00.1
    not
    a lightning bolt
    hummingbird's flutter
    wink of eye
    evil thought
    insight
    painlovedeath.
Only instruments do,
inevitably to lose themselves in their own world,
which may be the whole point,
shear time so fine
nothing human can be done
except lean an elbow
into their immortality.

**With the Famous Five on Parliament Hill:
Post Iraq Shock and Awe, 2004**

Standing among the Famous Five
as twilight rises on Parliament Hill
and the river below bends into dark,
I hear the sounds of war
rumbling up these bluffs.
Surely there was a Battle of Ottawa,
the French, the English crossing,
re-crossing the river,
scaling the heights, falling back,
if not here, somewhere.
So little ground free of blood,
so much history drained of spirit.

Canadian women
became persons in 1918
and seventy-one years later these Five
stand (and sit) monumentally on Parliament Hill.
Beyond Irene's winged hat, the full
and golden moon ascends and for a moment–
that's all there is.
I hug Henrietta,
her formidable flesh warm under bronze,
and touch Louise as tenderly as she holds
tea cup to cheek.
I bow to Emily who was "equal
to high and splendid braveries"
and to Nellie ever admonishing,
"Get the job done and let them howl."
That's the spirit!

The old moon, blazing white now,
fated companion of our oft times sorry history,
looks on
while the nation prepares to welcome
a war criminal.

Rights of the Person Corporate

I have the means, the motive, and the opportunity
to make you pay for the costs
of my profits—
black lung, acidic rising seas, carbonized biosphere.

I leap through loopholes of impunity,
surrounded by high walls of legal sleaze,
sentenced to life with immunity
by your conditioned ignorance.

I murder at will,
and dwell in maximum security.

If We're So Smart

Gravity waves arrived
on September 14, 2015.
Truth be known, they've always been arriving,
even before we did—
or another truth be known
they exist because we do—
little wrinkly things
shot from a cataclysmic 'collisionary' coitus
of two black holes which were
      GET THIS!
29 and 36 times more massive
than our sun—
occurring
1.3 billion years ago,
which in less than a second
      OH MY HEART!
was converted into ripplings
that generated a peak power output
fifty times that of
THE ENTIRE VISIBLE UNIVERSE!
      I KNOW, I KNOW, GET A GRIP!
Just listen,
because here, now in this poem
might be
your only chance to know
a gravity wave is passing through.
Einstein predicted them in 1916
but YO!
it took a century
before two Laser Interferometer Gravitational-Wave

Observatories—
one in Hanford, Washington and one in Livingston, Louisiana,
each with a four K long arm
and a right angle extension,
a kind of mammoth body snatcher,
as poets might say—
directly detected them,
making them real.
HERE'S THE KICKER;
these weary little guys,
zooming at the speed of light,
distort, wrinkle the very fabric of space/time, but
     YEP
remain undistorted themselves
     TRY THAT AT A HOCKEY GAME!
bringing pure information, what and how created,
oh, and where, which *we'll* never know.
Sit down, here now and
take your pulse and feel
the tinier-than-the-width-of-an-atomic-nucleus
pass through.
Between you and me,
dada data like this
bring on waves of dizzying ambivalence.
     IF WE'RE SO SMART
     WHY ARE WE SO GODAMN STUPID?!

Murder on the Internet

You're thirteen,
lovely reddish brown hair,
clear skin and bountiful heart,
but you must have made a terrible mistake
because drifting through the web
you appear
collaged in a tight dress (not yours),
"Anytime" written across swelling breasts (not yours)
that push up toward the sweetest smile (yours).

The trapdoor slams
and there is nothing familiar past or future,
all is present and tenuous
and that is the beginning.
Words fall, curl, dry up at the feet of this new real
and who (ever) has the hutzpah to
turn the tables at thirteen or
run to mama, when the forbidden
comes in your night dreams?

What is left
but www eyes and all eyes
imaging you at home & abroad,
self set in stone by others,
a commodity desired or spoiling on the shelf?
How can inwardness form
when what you feel, know, want
thins to no value out there,
nothing to face or face up to,
the weight of weightlessness
is who you are;
follow the logic out.

Election(s) November 2016

Shadows flee across the lawn
then flee again
the giant linden convulses.
In just enough light to see,
Leonard Cohen looks around,
"You want it darker…"
you got it
checks out
of the last hotel.

In These Times

I
"The answer, my friend,
is blowin' in the wind…"
So goes the old Dylan song
and it was
touching the lips of millions,
changing minds
but not the deep structures.
The same answer blows today
in ten thousand thousand
scraps of paper
ripped and scattered
on the winds of the world:
the harmattans, sciroccos, chinooks,
haboobs and monsoons.

II
Fault lines break out.
Whose fault?
Fissures bisect, trisect other fissures;
an unholy mess
of crossed s(word) interpretations
covering
a multitude of grievances,
each lone gun
a blade edge of history.
There's a vast sand mandala here,
exquisite in design
if you care to see it–
quick, though,
before it is slipped into the waters.

III
Wanted:
a racetrack bookie of renown
to set the odds on
which will come first,
    global banking crash   or   Civil War II USA,
        Earth heat at + 5 degrees   or   a nuclear missile attack,
    last elephant slaughtered   or   Bangladesh drowned,
        Cormac's "The Road"   or   Cormac's "The Road: Part Two"

The Last Luddite Addresses the Lonely Vapourized Crowd

The old Greeks emptied their unconscious
into a pantheon of gods,
who dutifully sported naked,
out of control in lust and revenge.
We do the same
with our avatars and virtual anonymities,
except
the ancients made art
while our wired world remakes us.

Remember when we had to kneel
in front of the TV to change channels,
which at least got us off the couch?
That honest genuflexion soon got replaced
by the very remote
illusion of control
and earth began to be
bound and wound tight with digital twine.

You feel this, don't you,
on some level,
as they say.

Space scared the hell
out of Pascal,
whose preoccupations went deeper
than "like,"
but maybe he'd have relaxed knowing
this fragile blue smallness
could be framed in a hand held thing.

Technology
surely takes our hands,
leading us through
a self-nullifying mantra;
"what can be done, should be done,"
and then further refined–
the human returns always diminishing.
We set things in motion,
they set us in motion (or demotion).

You feel it don't you,
how speed inhibits thought,
how keeping up with the world
according to apps
dismantles introspection?
Spam is maps.
They get us coming and going.
Digitalized instruments experience
unimaginably faster
what humans never can,
creating disposable, expendable us.

Leaping the gap from used to user,
might be the least of it.
Something's at work
and it's only partly us;
forgetting the difference
makes for unconscious spills everywhere.
Hell, we should know by now
death is at the bottom
of all our questions and quests,
mortality the hardest truth to live with,

denying it the substructure of art,
the well-wrought cup beside the corpse
and other evasions we name
God,
war,
even science.

Now that our species has become
death itself,
is it any wonder
we're blindly narcissistic
unable to recognize our own fate.
No biological evolution for millennia,
but something's driving us
and driving Earth to respond
with staggering retribution—
all over all over—
yet, we'd rather do anything than die.

You feel it, don't you?
the encroaching darkness swallowing us,
the sun rising on
a spent, slack-jawed, dazed humanity
facing the old, ever-futile choices:
flagellate others,
flagellate ourselves,
save ourselves no matter the cost,
accept the unacceptable
until the downward spiral grows tighter and tighter,
until the new old stars
witness another world made, unmade.
Beckett was right;
no final anything, on and on.

Let us, then,
those who have finally bowed our heads,
not to death rendering,
but surrendering to the supreme justice of it,
perform acts that feel right and lovely in themselves,
create profound, poignant, terrifyingly beautiful art,
make our lives ever-extending webs of love,
and, if we can,
let arise from the deepest recesses of our hearts
a tenuous trembling moment of gratitude
that we have lived at all.

For the Sheer Joy III

snow fell all night, all day, another night, a windless fall through zero revealing this January morning miniature polar bears asleep on every spruce bough, every deciduous branch doubled by its white shadow, the kiwi arbour tangled in stiff whipped cream, all motionless but for crow families flying to the sun and icy glass stars glinting on a snow sky.

Part V
Lines For Lines:
Five Poems & Eight Gestations

Prologue

for Tom Henderson

I entered the Galleria du Moncton in 2001 fully dressed, but little by little, as I gave myself to "Thirty Drawings and A Couple of Other Things," my cultural overlays were stripped away. I walked around naked for days. These life-sized charcoal and ink drawings of nude bodies on unframed white sheets jolted me out of my head into that existential bottom-line, the body. I was taken in by these powerful, visceral evocations of the body's capacity to express joy, to bear pain and isolation. It's the body that's crucified when the mind is in opposition to power. It's the body that orgasms and bleeds and trembles.

I had no choice. I went out to the studio of the creator of "Thirty Something", Tom Henderson, professor of art at Mount Allison University, and said, "I'd like to live with some of these for a while." Never known for taking meticulous care of his creations, Tom let me choose nine drawings, which he rolled and tied up, then slung into my car.

I carried the heavy sheets like a rug on my shoulder and released them onto the carpeted floor of my small basement writing room. I found no way in my cramped space to hang them so they remained crowded by book shelves, a large writing desk, a work table, and chairs. Dexterity was required in tiptoeing around them. When I was ready for a new drawing, I'd grasp with two hands the bottom of a sheet sometimes far down in the pile, pull it up until it was eye level, then spread it like a picnic cloth. Some of the edges that were torn before, became more so.

Then the long looking would begin, interrupted by my scribbling ideas. Sometimes the images exerted such power I had to turn away, take a walk. For several weeks, I lived with them. I admired and envied the directness with which the nude figures spoke their conditions. I let myself feel what they might be feeling and I wanted to crush the essence of these emotions into poetry. I think Tom and I worked from a common creative crucible of ambivalent, chaotic, erotic energy. Our thought was, one day, to hang the drawings and poems side by side. That has not happened. I decided to publish the poems alone with Tom's agreement. Thank you, Tom. These poems are dedicated to you; my lines for your lines.

Wo(man) Standing Serene

Where your head would be
daubs of pure white, spackling black space,
a Hubble photograph,
nebular mists pulled into galactic swirls,
or butterflies, flowers,
intercessions of joy, no matter.
Wo(man), your common belly
full of vapours recycled from original elements,
earth-plastered, dung heap visionary,
a strangeness out of strangeness.
A long, long journey
to nudge your soft cock pocking,
soft explosions in its head, pock, pock, pock
and clitoral lips open to the phasic moon.
Wo(man), earth-rooted, space-flung,
prick lifting into star shine,
cunt moistened in a bowl of celestial light.

Man and Woman on a Bed

It's finished for now.
                This is what we do.
We do it…
                to get it over with.
This is what we do
                We do it…
to get it over with.
                It's finished for now.

Baffled, resigned, the man hugs himself,
rude paws unable to trace the subtleties of love,
one eye shut, one gaped,
in retreat from lonely occupancy.
The woman's wiped out,
her narrow body ransacked,
a little bit of love
still clenched in her fists.

A few watery gray lines join them,
figures separately drawn,
spliced in spite of themselves.

Drawn to Tenderness

One muscled arm drops like a piston
splitting the nude figure down the middle.
Not easy to pull away from that powerful thrust
and take in the whole,
find the other arm cradling a small bundle.
Those smudged layers, angry, cross-hatched spaces
and that pile-driving arm,
all half-hearted subversions.
Drawing himself
through tumultuous ambivalence
is what must be done
to find tenderness
in that flesh sanctuary
of recessed power.

Standing Man Leaning Forward, Arms Outstretched, Head Hung

This is not Da Vinci's Vitruvian figure,
man as the measure, man *as* the universe,
touching all points of the globe with his magnificent form.
No, this body steels itself
against some enormous pressure;
if there's any heroism here
it's in the planted feet,
taking head-on the inevitable.
For all the nobility of ideas,
it's the body that's crucified.

Man and Woman with Wings

I
Let her go—
even if she drags those bedraggled wings
along the ground forever;
anything but this sheer, female endurance,
shame-hunched, obsequious,
waiting for something to pass.
But how *can* he?
having long ago blurred the line between
holding and holding down—
the cost, his enormous, unused wings.
And how can she even imagine
having freedom,
approached from the rear,
animal markers everywhere,
his muscled breastplate hot
against her back, power down-flowing
from radical beak through sinewy neck and shoulders;
how discern predator from protector.

II
It's an old species dream
to fly and be whole.
One of the last lessons will be
to fall
into forgetfulness
and meet randomly
like high circling hawks
playing
in the grace and daring of the other.

Eight Gestations

Frontal life-sized naked us
some turn away, mince sideways
profiling themselves

* * *

The odd foot disembodied
out of nowhere ready to strike
no pattern is the pattern

* * *

You keep us always naked
our hands too small
to cover the anguish

* * *

Closer to fur and darkness
than we think
cock-eyed and cruel

* * *

Split-tongued snake slips
from brain's base
we turn
facing an empty street

Purity does not exist
those who think so, deluded,
yet
we yearn for it

      *   *   *

What demons are exorcised
in the furious doing
on these sheets?

      *   *   *

Nothing titled, privileged, framed,
thirty something sheets hung in a row
poet dares to name

For the Sheer Joy IV

A sunflower cut in November, now brittled to lightness, lies face down on my desk, eight segmented lines run up the stem, make a right angle turn into a clutching muscle behind the eye, a miniature caramel volcano, clay, ochre-coloured lava flowing, fine white fuzzy-to-the-touch hairs bristle on stem and back of flower even to the sharp tips of wrinkled petals. I turn the sunflower over on her side, whirling out from around the dark brown pupil are bleached white seeds—each in its perfect socket—like a stunned school of fish.

Part VI
Foremothers

Foremothers

In Carlisle, Arkansas, May heat is withering.
I kissed your forehead and spoke of your goodness,
the year 2005, when I loosed a shovelful of earth
on the fact of your death,
but your long habitation in me
refused it...

All the mothers are gone now,
I leave poems, not children,
this one tracing and honouring
the maternal line.

I
Great-grandmother,
Emily Lucinda Henderson,
born between 1845 and 1848 in Tennessee
      in slavery times after the Indian Removal Act,
married in 1866 to James M. Quinton who was a private in the 11th Tennessee
      Volunteer Union Calvary, injured at Cumberland Gap, Virginia,
lived for a time in the Little Chunky area of Greene County, Tennessee,
      then on to Kentucky,
bore Louise, Clark, Mary,
      Oma, who "died at home in the kitchen fireplace,"
      Sermerimus, a name worthy of her own line,
      Beady, Claude, and a son who died in infancy and three unnamed ones,
died in 1928.

My memory of you is my mother's memory
of one childhood visit,
so I imagine
you seated on a stump, cheekbones high and coppery,

your gaze, steady, solemn, full of ancient wisdom
and the resignation that comes from having no use for it,
so little is known of you,
what matters is what I claim,
that fraction of half your blood,
"Cherokee"
a flame word
igniting ceremony and daring deeds,
and a pledge to your mythic foremothers
who walked across the Bering Land Bridge,
and all the women
whose struggles I made mine
and when deer call to me,
when I sequester myself to watch
or walk silent in the woods,
I want to believe
you are there.

So, I imagine
mother and child walking up a lane toward an old woman
who doesn't rise to greet them,
arms crossed, face lined and impassive.
There will be no broad gestures of affection.
"Ma, this here is Emily Frances, your granddaughter."
And when the rough hands reach out,
shy Emily of the gypsy-dark, sombre eyes moves forward,
"Well, come on in, y'all must be hongry."

Emily Lucinda,
did you know about
>	your Cherokee Nation with its own constitution,
>	the Indian Removal Act passed in 1830,

> the 7,000 troops led by Winfield Scott who forced your
> people off the land they had settled and farmed,
> the internment camp where your people died by the hundreds,
> about Nunna dual, the Trail Where They Cried?

Perhaps this sad history did not touch you,
you who came into womanhood in a border state in a nation divided by war
and lived into old age through yet another one tearing the world to pieces.
So little known, yet
how close you've always been.

II
Grandmother
Louise (sweet like the song, nicknamed "Lett,") Quinton Dennison,
born in 1867 in Tennessee to horse and buggy and mule-drawn plough
into stories of a civil war,
country-raised,
from your mother the striking cheekbones and quiet dignity,
life not to be questioned, but borne,
who found a good man, John Henry Dennison, when she was fifteen,
married in Barren County, Kentucky,
bore eight boys and three girls:
Clarence, who fathered four beautiful daughters,
Bessie Marie, my mother's favourite sister,
Floyd, who had mental problems and died of tuberculosis,
Walter, named "Cocky" for his crossed eye,
Kearney, my favourite uncle with the fine bass voice,
lovely Catherine "Tempie" who died of tuberculosis and had,
it was hinted, shadowy adventures,
Aubrey, musical, poetic, alcoholic, killed by the train he was riding somewhere,
Harry, who broke his back when drunk and died,
Paul and Shirley dead in infancy, and
Emily Frances who survived them all.

Grandmother,
I do not remember ever crawling into your lap,
but those childhood years, five to twelve,
nestled in your quiet, steady presence, no father around,
I do remember:
how you braided my hair too tight,
swabbed my throat with mercurochrome,
kept my infected foot in hot Epsom salts,
fried white mush, fried almost everything,
made a home while my mother worked,
and when I was sassy, how you
cut a switch from a tree and never caught me,
how you always carried a handkerchief,
which I later learned was for the snuff you dipped,
and that you couldn't read.
How your son, Aubrey, with the lovely high tenor voice,
would leave his hobo life and stay awhile,
our bedroom stinking of whiskey,
the kitchen full of song and
I remember coming to you with the kind of question
I still ask of the universe:
"Gramma, if I did this to God" thumbing my nose,
"would God see?"
"Yes, He would, but He would understand."
You didn't ask why I might want to do that.
I remember a story you told which made me wonder
if I could ever be as good,
of another granddaughter, baby Katherine Marie,
who seemed to know you had a swollen thumb
and lay still and angel-like under your hands and
I remember your softly urgent voice at the bathroom door,

"Marilyn, President Roosevelt is dead." And
how the world shifted for us.
And when the second stroke carried you off
on July 4 a few years later, I remember
how mother rose from her seat as the casket lid closed
screaming "Mama, Mama."
Suddenly the buffer between us,
and the prop we both leaned on fell away
and we were thrown together,
depending, off-balance.

Peasant stock,
farming people,
mostly illiterate,
out of the south,
moving northward
with the times to work,
Scots-Irish,
Cherokee.

And Emily Frances
who survived them all.

III
All the mothers are gone now,
I leave poems, not children.

May heat in Carlisle, Arkansas is withering,
but there's mason jars of iced tea at Adveda's,
quail, biscuits and gravy for breakfast,
there are armadillos cracked open on old highway 70,
cotton mouth moccasins in the ditches,
new green shoots of rice on curving levees,

and in Emmanuel Baptist Church,
the casket cool and full with your stillness.
Later in a place called Snake Island,
I loosed a shovelful of earth on the fact of your death,
but your long habitation in me
refused it.

When she was in her eighties and the dementia setting in, I wrote,
"I do not know what I will be when she is gone, when *us* does not exist.
Even as her brain begins to tangle, even in this diminished state,
somehow her existence
keeps me alive."

For a few years more in the nursing home,
she'd swing her hips, "Get down, Miz Frances,"
reach toward any child, sing in tune,
live on Ensure for two years,
take to diapers and a wheelchair,
kick the aides and grin, make a fist,
enjoy sunsets at the end of the corridor,
rise at 2 a.m. to report
"A man's after my virginity",
become singular and loved.

Her voice from the nursing home,
"I wish we could be young together."

…got as far as Denver,
its International Airport soars,
and I was ready to fly home,
after three weeks away,
after seeing my mother into the ground…
I wanted to go home

*but was stopped in my tracks—
not sudden pain or faintness, but
simply not my self,
I wanted to go home,
but was loaded into an ambulance instead.*

Mother, Emily Frances, last of eleven,
born out of a weary womb in 1910, who
lost her beloved pa when she was twelve,
sought and never found another,
twice married, once to a man obscurely absent,
my father, who did not provide
and another who was wounded and
could not love without hurting.

Much younger, you told a friend, his was the best sex
you had ever had,
a hard worker, could provide,
so, lonely and unaware,
you married a man who had never divorced his first wife
and who never offered to adopt your daughter.

Two weeks,
happy in her happiness,
released to mine.
Two weeks
and then he turned on her.
A time to learn how much loneliness
I could bear,
adolescence coincident
with an ear pressed against the wall,
hearing sounds of a new and rough allegiance,
odd child out,

moon my essential companion
resplendent in light not its own.
For six years, it was like this:
my body a monolith of hatred,
shut down and numb,
ever fearful of catalyzing harm,
peace
dependent on
how much she was willing to give up,
her weakness, by extension, mine.
Arms once flung open to the sun,
closed in fierce self-holding,
no touching, no affection among us,
lulls of pretence but mostly
each on edge, watching for signs,
he for any excuse to rage and stifle her,
she for how he came in the door,
what she saw in my eyes.
Broken glass underfoot and
no one to sweep it up.

There's a place
the ancient Greeks called third voice,
a force field
where two pervade each other.
I wanted to go home
but was stopped in my tracks.

Underground,
angels and demons entwined in rapt embrace
would take a lifetime to disentangle,
massive doses of pain sought and inflicted

to feel anything,
and a bedrock trust,
I'd be all right.
Waking one morning in my father's living room
on a fold-up bed,
mother gone forever into her life,
I, seventeen, and never relieved of her,
stomach unclenched,
breathing freely,
first time in six years.

A car sideswiped the ambulance.
I was removed to a grassy knoll
in the middle of crazy eight interstate exits,
and left
staring at the sky
where I was supposed to be.
Kerreeist,
they have to make a police report!

I remember how
on the verge of another relationship gone bad,
I grasped my mother to me awkwardly
"All I ever wanted was your love"
meaning also
all I ever wanted was to love her purely,
without ambivalence,
remembering how her guilt and shame
kept her unworthy to ask anything of me
and how mine kept me unworthy even to forgive,
our love preserved
in mutual relinquishment.

It's
the flush of warmth
released
whenever I turn in the hospital bed
the modulated slow drip into my veins
the air cool in my nostrils
that allow in
a muted fear
I'd never see home

Mother,
who loved to laugh and tease, sing, play catch,
stand among cows and feel the evening close,
who worked in the fields those years in Arkansas,
a farmer's wife, strong of body,
kicked only once by him,
and though things got better never
freely loved or loving,
chopping cotton, hauling water, driving tractors,
who killed with a shovel rattlesnakes,
and cooked for a pack of hounds,
who carried soup and casseroles to shut-ins,
prayed and was lonely often,
who suffered without becoming bitter,
and who fearlessly with me
unravelled the strands of the tight braid
that was our life,
each owning our own,
then tenderly, carefully, hand over hand,
braided them again.

It's the
cool air flowing
through transparent tubing
blissful
being breathed
that lets the letting go begin.

Once, sitting in the pre-dawn dark of her kitchen,
the car packed for leaving,
as always in the last hour,
we try to say everything, leave everything perfect
between us.
We remember, it's the 4th of July,
and she tells a story I had not heard before:
"I sat holding her hand. She was slipping away.
I bent over her and my last words,
'Mother, do you love me?'"
She looked at me across the table,
her eyes brimming with tears of disbelief,
"All I ever wanted was her love."
And there, shimmering in the air between us,
the third voice of
our desperate, insatiable love,
handed down mother to daughter.
I drove seventeen hours straight,
her words soft mallet-mantra taps
in the brain, in the rhythm of the tires
rolling from Carlisle to Memphis, across Tennessee,
through Virginia and home:
everything is as it had to be
everything is as it had to be.

I couldn't leave until
in night's deep center
my partner on her hard cot also aware,
a presence enters the room,
moving soundlessly in dim bluish light,
adjusts the cool flow of oxygen
with gentleness beyond earthly,
stays with my eyes a long moment,
then gone
and I released.

October 16, 2010,
Mother, your one-hundredth birthday
if you had lived, always
in my memory and heart,
in my eyes and strong legs,
I bow to you and carry on.

For the Sheer Joy V

Sheer Joy
is when,
gazing long enough at what is other–
> one lavender cosmos pressing against the window,
> eight satiny transparent petals
> in a gentle clutch of green, yellow eyes beaded and seeded–

it comes to be fully present, presenting beyond subject/object,
imagination in stone, water, in thought.

Sheer Joy
is when
gazing long enough, expectant without expectations, like the sudden dip
of a divining rod,
hollowed rock is
an open, empty violin case lined with shredded orange pine cone.

Sheer joy
is
what lovers create, a mystical thirdness;
what we make of and in the world, what the world makes of and in us,
all and ever a conditioned arising.

Note

My cousin, Wanda Kelly, Louisville, Kentucky, became our family's historian. A large portion of the facts about our foremothers' lives comes from her diligent research and is greatly appreciated. I claim sole responsibility for the use of those facts.

Acknowledgements

Working with Keith Helmuth and Brendan Helmuth, of Chapel Street Editions, has been a most amiable and absorbing experience from beginning to end. Keith's editing eye caught much that the poet overlooked and his suggestions always made way for improvements. We discovered, along with our love of poetry, that we both had been among the thousands of Vietnam antiwar protesters tear-gassed outside the 1968 Democratic National Convention in Chicago. Brendan's artistic sense of book and cover design takes the text to heart, for which I am also grateful.

About the Author

Marilyn Lerch has authored four collections of poetry, including *Lambs & Lamas, Ewes & Me* (2001), *Moon Loves Its Light* (2005), *Witness & Resist* (2008), and *The Physics of Allowable Sway* (2013). From 2014 to 2018, she served two terms as Sackville, New Brunswick's Poet Laureate. She was president of the Writers' Federation of New Brunswick from 2006 to 2010. For twenty-four years, starting in 1967, she taught in the Washington, D.C. Public Schools and participated in many anti-imperial, gay and women's movements. She is a Canadian citizen and has lived in Sackville with her partner, Janet, since 1996. Her travels have taken her to Greece, Turkey, Nepal, Kashmir, Bali, France, Spain, Italy, Nicaragua, and El Salvador.

www.ingramcontent.com/pod-product-compliance
Lightning Source LLC
Chambersburg PA
CBHW060534080526
44586CB00012B/734